Letters from Lockdown

About the Contributors

Claire Foster-Gilbert is the founder director of Westminster Abbey Institute. A public philosopher and author, Foster-Gilbert has played an instrumental role in the fields of medical research ethics and environmental issues.

Treena Fleming is a Detective Chief Superintendent in the Metropolitan Police Service. She has been the local police Commander for North Area Basic Command Unit, which incorporates the London boroughs of Enfield and Haringey, since April 2019.

Dawn Butler is a Labour Member of Parliament for the constituency of Brent Central. She is a former Shadow Equalities Minister and made history as the first African-Caribbean female MP to hold a position as minister in the UK.

Peter Howitt is a senior civil servant. He is Incident Director in the Department of Health and Social Care and an Honorary Fellow and Lecturer at the Centre for Health Policy, Imperial College London.

LETTERS FROM LOCKDOWN

Sustaining Public Service Values
During the Covid-19 Pandemic

Claire Foster-Gilbert, Treena Fleming,
Dawn Butler and Peter Howitt

First published by Haus Publishing in 2020
4 Cinnamon Row
London SW11 3TW
www.hauspublishing.com

A CIP catalogue record for this book is
available from the British Library

Print ISBN: 978-1-913368-05-0
Ebook ISBN: 978-1-913368-06-7

Typeset in Arno by MacGuru Ltd

Printed in the United Kingdom by Clays Elcograf S.p.A

Contents

Acknowledgements

Our sincere thanks go to the Dean and Chapter of Westminster, the Steering Group, Council of Reference and Fellows of Westminster Abbey Institute, Alison Bean, Ruth Cairns, Harry Hall, Alice Horne, Aneta Horniak, Susan Howitt, Kathleen James, Seán Moore, Clare Moriarty, Barbara Schwepcke and Sunbeam House in Hastings.

Introduction

Claire Foster-Gilbert

How do public servants respond to a global challenge that
doesn't look like anything they have seen before? Protocols
and preparations have to be adopted and quickly adapted,
decisions made and articulated clearly in the midst of many
unknowable factors, steady, reliable leadership established,
and more. Much more.

Of the public servants with whom Westminster Abbey
Institute works – politicians, civil servants, uniformed service
personnel, journalists, educationalists, ministers of religion,
scientists, artists and others – some have been very much
in evidence during the pandemic, working excessive hours,
pushed to the limits of their capacity, while others are unob-
trusively working equally punishing and intense hours from
home. Still others have been, for one good reason or another,
apparently unable to contribute. About to return to work after
cancer treatment, I myself was placed in that category of vulnerable people who had to shield themselves for at least twelve
weeks. The Institute seeks to sustain public service values, and
it seemed to me that that offering was needed now more than
ever. My desire to launch into action was entirely frustrated, so
I mobilised the written word.

The first 'Letter from Lockdown', addressed to the Institute's core community of Fellows and Council of Reference,* was sent on 27 March. I sought to give voice to their circumstances and to strengthen the motivation that each of them feels to serve the public. Each week, for five weeks, it became possible to write something without knowing beforehand what it would be or whether there would be another letter the following week. By the sixth letter, a narrative was emerging out of the unfolding events and the letters found a corresponding shape and content: to strengthen the souls not just of the Institute's core community but of all those seeking to navigate our country through the consequences of the coronavirus. The letters became more structured, pedagogic and public. More by intuition than rational judgement, I decided that twelve letters would be the right number. The fact that, in retrospect, they seem to follow a narrative and to come to an end at the same time as an identifiable episode – the intense lockdown period – is not due to my prophetic ability. Like all of us, I was watching and responding from a state of not knowing. All I really understood was that it was right to try to keep faith with Westminster Abbey's neighbours with a regular pulse of goodwill and support, to sustain the public service values that so vitally underpin the response to a crisis like the Covid-19 pandemic.

* Westminster Abbey Institute's Council of Reference is an advisory board of senior public servants. Details of members can be found at www.westminster-abbey.org/institute/institute-people. The Fellows are graduates of the Institute's Fellows' Programme for public servants entering senior roles. Details and further information about the Programme can be found at www.westminster-abbey.org/institute/fellows-programme.

The letters, reproduced here, are intended to be inspiring, not critical. Their content is predicated on the belief that if you call out of a well-motivated person the best that is in them, they are more likely to believe in themselves and offer their best, even as circumstances get tough. This is at the heart of how Westminster Abbey Institute operates: it does not comment on policy or criticise policymakers; it does not campaign for specific causes. It seeks, rather, to encourage what is good in our public servants, nurturing their vocations to service, promoting public service values, and kindling the moral and spiritual values that ensure the service is sustained and endures. But this is no comfortable option. At the heart of public service values are truth and truth telling. The letters are followed by reflections from three of the Institute's Fellows: a police officer, an MP and a civil servant, each of whom writes their own, sometimes hard to hear, truth.

Heaven knows, and the Fellows' reflections show, support and encouragement were needed. Individuals were working long hours – some physically on the frontline, some from home, some juggling childcare alongside availability to respond at all hours, facing all the same constraints and challenges the public they serve was facing. Public service institutions' systems of working were being tested like never before, as was the whole ecology of public service itself, the vital connectivity across institutions and between the people within them.

By its nature, much of what faces public servants during the pandemic was, and will be, unforeseeable. The nature of the virus itself is still being investigated and understood. Such unknowability demands nimble responses. These in turn demand that the inner mindset and core values of a person and an institution are strong and well exercised, ready to face the unknown and not to be thrown off balance by it. The letters sought to address and strengthen the inner core, offering a kind of Pilates for the soul.

A Hero's Journey?

One way of making sense of the still-unfolding story of the pandemic is to map it on to the classic 'hero's journey', articulated by Joseph Campbell and referred to in the letters. In the hero's journey, the word 'hero' simply means 'protagonist': the person at the centre of the story who responds to the call to embark on a quest and who is invariably changed by it. Many of the public servant key workers in the pandemic are rightly called heroes, but the letters recognise that those who are forced by circumstances *not* to act are also heroes in the story. Their service lies in staying still, above all in not getting themselves infected. These perform the quiet sacrifice of domestic, quotidian heroism that is all the more remarkable as time passes. And as the story of the pandemic unfolds, it becomes clear that its 'hero' is all of us.

In the hero's journey, the main protagonists are assailed by a call that wakes them up, shaking them out of their ordinary world and all its assumptions. The call can come from inside them or from outside. For us, the pandemic was a call from outside, as it spread across the globe and woke us all up from our ordinary worlds of busy distraction, attention to what we thought was important – and *was* important, then. But the protagonists at first resist the call: really, we are fine and safe as we are, do we have to leave our ordinary worlds? Is this a true call or one that we can safely ignore? It was a true call. Whole nations were returning to their homes, if they were lucky enough to have them, and closing the doors behind them. The UK followed suit. On 25 March, the Coronavirus Act 2020 received Royal Assent and the population was instructed to stay at home for three weeks, only leaving the house for essential shopping and exercise. Those of us in the most vulnerable category should not leave the house for any reason. Only key workers could leave their homes to work. In the classic story, this is the point at which the call to leave the ordinary world is followed, the protagonists cross the threshold, and the journey begins. In our pandemic story, the threshold was sometimes crossed to go out into a world that had become newly fearsome or, paradoxically, it was crossed to stay back, in a home that no longer looked ordinary. For many public servants – MPs and civil servants included – home became the location for their greatest service. The first letter speaks of this diversity of response to the call.

Once the journey is underway, the protagonists face many challenges: trials that they find ways to overcome, learning as they go, because many of the trials are not ones they have faced before. Mistakes are made. The journey and its destination only start to emerge from the mists surrounding them as the protagonists move towards them, and they continually confound their expectations. In our story, March moved into April and unexpectedly hot weather tested the patience of a population urged to stay inside. The death toll started to rise and fear spread, keeping the protagonists focused. It seemed to me that our public servants were playing a symphony of service in music that was only being written moments before it had to be performed, and I wrote as much in the second letter. Each had their part to play in the ensemble; it was important to keep playing, even if a fellow player faltered for any reason; it mattered that no one tried to take over the whole piece but recognised the interdependence of every part. Improvised music had to happen within the context of the whole emerging composition. We had to trust each other.

And in all the great journeys, there is a time of great darkness and difficulty, a 'great ordeal' that tests the protagonists to their utmost. In our journey, the great ordeal fell over the Easter weekend in mid-April, though we did not know at the time that it was the peak. The third letter was written as we collectively entered the darkness. The reported death toll rose to more than 10,000. The NHS faced its greatest challenge, as hospital admissions rose and kept on rising. Healthcare workers and carers were pushed to their limits of service, struggling to restore lives and accompany lonely deaths. The pain of families unable to see their ailing and dying loved ones in hospitals and care homes was palpable. The prime minister, in hospital himself with Covid-19, was moved into intensive care.

The fourth letter observed that while the much-used metaphor of fighting a battle was understandable, in fact we met the great ordeal not with war, but with love.

Part of the ordeal was that we did not know whether worse was to come and the limits we had reached would be pushed even further. When you are reading a book or watching a film, you can work out where you are in the story because you know when it is going to end. Not so for us at this time, as the sixth letter noted.

And so we worked on through the challenges and trials as the journey unfolded. The letters took on the pedagogic task of teaching public servants how to strengthen their souls so they could draw deeply on inner resources for the kind of energy that endures. The death toll continued to rise but less steeply, and gradually we emerged to a place where we could say, not entirely confidently, that the first wave of the virus was at last receding. In the classic story, the protagonists take a moment to draw breath and let themselves *feel* what they have been through. The hero's journey is transformative. No one emerges untouched. Tough as it might have been, Joseph Campbell writes of gaining the 'elixir', which is the real goal of the quest, only recognised when it is encountered deep within oneself and in one's fellow travellers, and only revealing itself when the journey is undertaken, never beforehand. With the elixir comes the possibility of a new level of life, with fresh journeys to undertake but with protagonists who are stronger and wiser: the journeys are different, and they are changed. The last letter reflected on this transition and invited public servants to acknowledge the powerful inner resources they had discovered by means of this first part of the journey. We don't yet know what the consequences of the pandemic are; we don't know what the world will be even in the next six months, let alone next year or in the decades to come. But we can and should acknowledge the qualities of compassionate service that have been called upon and continually exercised on the journey so far. These are available to us as we face the uncertain times to come. They can also play their part in *determining* what is to come. On a very personal note, it is my own experience of living with incurable cancer that has started to teach me this, and I wanted to pass on what I am learning about the ongoing, unknown journey.

The Post-heroic Journey

For many of us, our experience of the last three months has not been like a journey at all. It has rather been an anti-journey, a restraint on movement, an enforced stillness that has made us, often unwillingly, take a steady and protracted look at all that we are and have been striving for. There is another storyline to describe this experience: the 'post-heroic'.* In this story, there are no departures to new worlds, no great conquests or trials. Rather, the heroes are undone by some sort of downfall, perhaps through hubris as a result of their previous, triumph-ant journeys. Something challenges them and turns their world upside down. They are forced to discover what really matters to them, what they cannot afford to lose when everything is threatened. This story too has its hopeful outcomes, as we reevaluate everything we have been so busy working at, redis-cover what matters more than anything to us and reconnect with that, leaving what is now unimportant to one side. The fifth letter addresses the question of humanity's future: as we pass through the canyon of stresses brought on at least partly by our hubristic belief we could control nature, how will we be

* The post-heroic journey is a counter-narrative to Campbell's, suggested by those who think he does not sufficiently account for much human experience. For a good discussion of this, see Peter Reason, *In Search of Grace: An Ecological Pilgrimage* (Alresford, Hampshire, John Hunt Publishing, 2017) pp. 146–149.

when we emerge? Compassionate, or competitive? Those who have been working punishing schedules to meet the needs of the pandemic have not had a moment to look up and see the world that their deep service has been creating. But those who have been in the enforced stillness of the post-heroic journey can stand witness to their service and staunchly defend the compassion that underlies it, that we want to retain when we have come through the rapids to a new world.

Inner Depth and Interdependence

Two other images that feature in the letters are worthy of attention and reflection. One, in the fourth letter, is that of a three-legged race. Tied to each other, the competitors cannot simply run selfishly towards their own personal goals, relying only on their own strength and skill. The people who make a connected couple have to tune in, each to the other, and find a pace and rhythm that suits both. That connectedness becomes more important than winning the race: without it, both will stumble and fall, and the race will be lost as well as much else besides. In this letter, I suggest that the little tie that binds the couple's ankles together is love. Love was the prime minister's discovery in his own great ordeal as he spent 48 hours in intensive care with his life in the balance. The care and compassion that have been incarnated by so many during the last twelve weeks is this: love.

The other image, in the sixth letter, is of an arrow let fly from the archer's bow – but only after it has been drawn right back. In the analogy, the arrow is public service. The further back the archer, the public servant, is able to draw the bow, the further and more truly the arrow will fly. Drawing the bow back means giving oneself the space and time to cultivate and prepare one's inner life, to make oneself as ready as one can be to face the unknown challenges that are coming at us now.

Following the letters are three reflections by three public servants, Fellows of Westminster Abbey Institute, describing their different experiences of the pandemic. Detective Chief Superintendent Treena Fleming of the Metropolitan Police, the Commander responsible for the boroughs of Enfield and Haringey, writes movingly of the unfailing service she witnessed in her officers, whose stoical attitude masked the sacrifices they were making. She writes that it was their attitude that enabled her to overcome any personal concerns as she stepped daily into her critical leadership role, determinedly making herself a visible example of responsive resilience. Dawn Butler MP writes with searing honesty of the pain she experienced, daily assailed by wave after wave of grief suffered by her constituents, her staff and her own family, compounded by an increase in the abusive online attacks to which she is subject as a black woman MP and culminating, when she was already overloaded with pain, with the killing of George Floyd and its reawakening of the traumatic racist abuse that her own family has suffered in the past. In her reflection, she turns the pain into challenging questions for us all about ongoing systemic and systematic racism. She thus calls into play the need identified in the eleventh letter for institutions to attend to their hidden, unhealthy stories, and in the seventh letter to ensure that diverse perspectives inform and challenge our unconscious assumptions. Finally, Peter Howitt, senior civil servant in the Department of Health and Social Care, found himself not individually but collectively vitally important, as one of a symphony of a hundred civil servants working in shifts, simultaneously juggling childcare and all the other challenges of lockdown. Each member of the Department's Incident Response Team played their part in the ensemble and thus ensured unbroken service, collecting and providing data, negotiating to bring people home from abroad, and delivering quantities of complex, detailed guidance that stemmed from the policies daily announced by government ministers.

Just as every hero's journey ends up being not about the solo main protagonist but about everyone else, so these letters and reflections arose not solely from their authors but out of communities. Treena Fleming knew how much her service emerged not through her but through her officers. Dawn Butler recognised from the outset how critical her staff were and how much she needed to support them as they struggled to serve her from their places of isolation. Peter Howitt saw the symphony, not the singularity, of his work. In turn, the letters published here are the product of many conversations and years of research and practice. I am indebted, in particular, to Clare Moriarty who read each letter and gave critical feedback from her long and distinguished experience in government. Comments and support from Reverend Dr James Hawkey and Paul Baumann of the Institute's Steering Group influenced the letters' content. The listening community of Institute Fellows and Council of Reference and the wider community of public servants provided the inspiration to write the letters. I want, especially, to thank Institute Fellows the Venerable Liz

Adekunle, Detective Chief Superintendent Steve Clayman and Cathy Millar for their advice. And there would have been no point in putting pen to paper were not the Institute team and Haus Publishing able to ensure the letters got to where they were needed. My profound thanks go to you all.

Letter one: 27 March 2020

Stillness is service too

Dear Friends,

I find, to my utter chagrin, that I am 'extremely vulnerable'. Along with many of my fellow vulnerables, I received a text on Monday morning, telling me that my underlying condition means that Covid-19 is a serious threat to my life, and I have to shield myself from external sources of infection for twelve weeks.

I am not happy being in the group that needs help. All my life, I have thought of myself as among those who make a difference, who care, who serve, who lead people to better worlds. I help others, they don't help me. It grates.

But I have to accept that the precise means of my service now is just this: to not get ill. It's a negative act, a non-act. I have to stay still.

And as I practise staying still, I discover how addicted I am to being that person who is so active in the service of others. Who, if I'm completely honest, needs to hear others tell me I have made a difference to them if my self-esteem, even my sense of identity, is to be affirmed.

I have to find a different way to be of service now. Even if I do, it is unlikely to be noticed or rewarded.

In your different spheres of parliament, government, law enforcement, defence, teaching, research, healthcare, journalism, art, care of souls, and more, you are working flat out, serving the nation in its time of need. I picture you borne aloft by your public service values like never before, finding resources of strength, resilience, responsiveness, flexibility, percipience and profound care. I am in awe and admiration of your spirit, and I send you my deepest goodwill.

There will be others of you who have all those qualities and for one infuriatingly valid reason or another are not able to manifest them in the same highly demanding way. I am in awe and admiration of you, too.

Our common longing to roll up our sleeves and get active is evident in the magnificent, widespread and generous response to the call for volunteers to help the NHS. It is heartening to see how fundamentally decent humanity can be in its instinctive move to protect the weak.

But what is the service those of us who are obliged to stay still can offer?

Loss of stillness can mean loss of balance, perception and energy. So we who are forced to not-act must find the stillness in our own hearts and at the heart of our nation, and magnify it. We have to learn how much, how very badly, we all need it. We have to know that staying still is service too.

You are in our thoughts and prayers.

With love,
Claire

Letter two: 3 April 2020

Harmony and dissonance

Dear Friends,

I offer this image for our time of need: public service is like a vast orchestra and choir performing a magnificent, entirely new piece of music. Everybody has a different part to sing or play, sometimes together, sometimes solo. Some people, like the violinists or the drummers, are playing fast and frantically for much of the piece. Others, like the cymbal player, play loudly and effectively, but only occasionally. The choir lifts its voice at times, then falls silent and sits down.

There is harmonic unity: civil servants delivering the stark, dramatic announcements of the prime minister and other ministers, or teams working together to create the Nightingale Hospitals. There is harmonic tension: journalists calling politicians to account, civil servants giving difficult advice to ministers or parliament scrutinising government.

The music is affected if anyone, anxious to be active when they should be still, tries to sing or play the part of another. If someone loses their place and falters into unintended silence, perhaps losing heart or falling ill and having to withdraw for a bit, the greatest help their fellow performers can give is to continue to play steadily on until they find their place again and rejoin the performance.

Performers must forgive each other when they play wrong

notes or sing out of turn. After all, the score is being written barely moments before it is performed. Courage and confidence are key. Listening is key. Staying in tune with each other is key.

Music isn't music until it is performed and heard. The audience – the public – is part of the music too. Sound meets listening; public service meets public need. Only in that encounter, at that moment, does the performance or the public service come to life.

From where you are sitting, you may hear the harmony around you, in your care home or hospital or government department or police borough or armed forces deployment area or cabinet or constituency or news outlet. You may hear a distant roar that is part of the composition, but you cannot make it out or connect with it. You may hear only dissonance.

You may not hear the harmony, yet. But you are all facing in the same direction and following the same baton: public service.

From the stillness of my shielded state, I can hear harmony. Please keep playing this new music for us all.

You continue in our thoughts and prayers.

With love,
Claire

Letter three: 9 April 2020

Into the darkness

Dear Friends,

The vast orchestra and choir of public servants play on, but the prime minister, their conductor, has been taken into hospital. Despite his absence, our mature democracy and evolved constitution mean that the parts can keep playing, still facing in the same direction: public service in all its forms seeking to protect life.

The foreign secretary picks up the baton. The score, for now, is written and agreed: repeat the refrain to stay at home; keep building intensive care capacity; keep increasing tests for the virus; keep on with clinical trials for a vaccine against it. But circumstances may change at any time. And although the symphony is still playing, it is getting harder for performers and audience alike. Adrenalin is not good fuel for a long haul, and what do we run on when it has subsided? Will the public settle in and find ways of relishing the lockdown? Or will resentment and stress boil up?

Health and social care workers are confined too, in claustrophobic personal protective equipment. Vital though it is, it adds to the physical barriers between carers and their patients, while the deepest personal questions of all are beginning to press: who is going to live? Will we have to choose who will be left to die? How will I accompany you, as you face your own mortality? What is there to say or do, when medicine can no longer keep you alive and your loved ones are not here?

The conductor, the prime minister, has joined the ranks of patients in hospital. He has become a still point at the political heart of our nation. Boris 'the fighter' can, for a time, no longer rely on his body to be and do what he wants it to. For a time, his body has to stay still. He has to concentrate on one thing only: to breathe. His life is reduced to its essence.

In facing death, Mr Johnson has become one with every Covid-19 patient taken into intensive care. Each is offered the opportunity to plumb the depths of the darkest mystery: that our lives will come to an end one day. Each patient can, for a time, surrender all ambition, give up the projected life story, the assumed destiny and accoutrements of a successful human being, and receive, in their place, what is left when they have all departed.

Not absence. Nor despair, nor fear.

If the patients in intensive care can allow themselves to go to that place of greatest fallibility and not be distracted – and if they survive – they will emerge stronger and wiser than before. How we go into our own dark depths determines who we are when we emerge.

As with the Covid-19 patients in intensive care, so with all of us. We are collectively walking through a deep darkness made of fear of the unknown, facing our own mortality, facing our own weakness, some of us active beyond measure, some of us passive, shielded from infection, but not shielded from the most difficult questions of all. How we go through our darkness will determine how we emerge: weakened, or wiser and ready to adapt to a different world.

In the Christian story of Easter, which is upon us, there is resurrection – the triumph of love – but not before the crucifixion, not unless there's an entry into darkness first.

You continue in our thoughts and prayers.

With love,
Claire

Letter four: 17 April 2020

Finding love

Dear Friends,

Last week, I suggested that when everything you think you are has been stripped away, you do not find mere absence, and nor do you find despair, nor fear. I didn't say what you do meet, because I was writing about the prime minister – representing as he did all Covid-19 patients in intensive care – and only he could say what happened when his life hung in the balance. I know what I met, in the awful stripped-down days of absolute weakness and vulnerability when my bone marrow, and all the bacteria in my gut, had been destroyed, and my stem cell transplant hadn't yet grafted. But that is my story.

We now know what Mr Johnson came face to face with during those critical 48 hours, because he told us. It was love. And he said that was what made the NHS unconquerable, that was what would bring it and all of us through this time.

Love. Not war.

We are using a lot of war metaphors at the moment, understandably, because we are in a crisis. We will combat this disease; we will fight this virus; we will destroy it; we will be triumphant. Our battle cries unite us against a common foe, stirring our sinews, goading our wills to win.

But those of us who have to stay shielded or are furloughed

are goaded only into frustration because we can't act. And even you who are in the thick of it are not rushing around shouting and lopping off heads.

You who are right on the forefront, actually facing the virus itself, are sitting stock still and observant in your laboratories, looking through microscopes, carefully researching tests and vaccines, your quiet patience essential if reliable results are to be produced.

You healthcare workers attending to patients are a calm, strong, reassuring presence: fighting is not the word for what you are doing, as you monitor the breathing of the sick, or gently turn their bodies to ease their lungs. You may be accompanying your patient into death, and what place does a battle metaphor have there, when you must allow a life to be surrendered and *not* call it failure?

You politicians leading the nation have to do so with calm steadfastness. You civil servants delivering the policies so swiftly brought into being by ministers need to sustain your clear thinking, be wide awake to unthought-of consequences and their potential hazards even as the world is drawn to the main challenge of the virus. You law enforcers need to act firmly but gently, winning consensus from the public you protect. You journalists must report truthfully without whipping up fear.

The name for what all of you are doing is this: care. Care is the expression of love.

In a three-legged race, there is a goal to achieve: to win the race. But you have to pay attention to your partnership almost more than winning. You stay together, and together you increase your speed. The moment you forget you are attached, you both tumble. The little tie attaching our ankles is made of love, if we could only see it. Mr Johnson did.

You continue in our thoughts and prayers.

With love,
Claire

Letter five: 24 April 2020

Still shooting the rapids

Dear Friends,

Love, not war, underlies our narrative of public service. That was last week's discovery.

So if the bewildering story we are living through is not one of vanquishing the enemy, what is it? What does it mean for a narrative's forward movement to be powered by love?

In the myth of Triptolemus, the gift of wheat made settled communities possible as farming, not hunting, became humanity's main source of food. With more time to spare and a stable place to experiment, we learned many skills and, ultimately, so it seemed, established ourselves at the top of the food chain. But the gift of wheat was a curse as well as a blessing. By the end of the twentieth century, we had become a rogue species, the wrong kind of lords of the universe. Unwittingly, we poisoned the planet as never before, harming every sphere: the atmosphere, the hydrosphere, the lithosphere, the pedosphere and the biosphere.

We are not lords of the universe, and we are not top of the food chain. We have always been part of the cycle of nature. We still have predators: they are microorganisms like the coronavirus, effective because it can't be seen with the naked eye, because it mutates and dances around and through us faster than we can track and trace, faster than we can prevent. And other threats, like hurricanes and storms and droughts, are not holding back until we say that we're ready to cope with them.

James Martin predicted that the twenty-first century would see humanity pass through multiple crises in short order, like a boat navigating a narrow canyon, and we are certainly shooting the rapids now.* Those of you who have the daily fast-moving responsibility to deliver help to where it is needed have to concentrate on that. You are, to continue the analogy, variously at the front of the boat trying to see what is coming, at the helm trying to steer, at the side paddling to keep the boat moving and prevent it from being punctured by the rocks that everywhere threaten, or tending to the sick passengers. You are simply responding to the situation as it presents itself, and that is where your energy is focused. It's an expression of love like never before.

Those of us who can't so actively help are sitting or lying in the middle of the boat allowing ourselves to be carried in this heroic way. We place our trust in our crew. We cheer you on with all our hearts. And we, too, have a job to do. On behalf of all humanity, we can absorb the shock we have been administered and learn from it. In our enforced quietude we can prepare ourselves to be the people we need to be when the boat emerges on the other side of the canyon.

Compassionate, not merciless. Part of nature, not dominating it.

* James Martin, *The Meaning of the 21st Century: A vital blueprint for ensuring our future* (London, Random House, 2007).

Let this crisis transform enough of us. Let the love underlying our narrative keep showing.

You continue in our thoughts and prayers.

With love,
Claire

Enduring the journey by strengthening the soul

Dear Friends,

In all the great stories, protagonists embark upon a quest. They cross the threshold into the unknown, face trials, make mistakes, find mentors and companions, go through a time of darkness when everything has gone wrong and everyone has deserted them, face a great ordeal that tests all that they have and are, and emerge into a new level of life, transformed by the journey. Most of the challenges and tests of our lives, though unique in their particulars, follow a similar arc, and looking back, it can be possible to see how we have moved through such journeys, long and short, great and small, and been formed by them.

When you are in the middle of a story, however, it's difficult to see where you are or make much sense of the narrative arc. You are just going through the story. Is this the threshold of a new journey, or just another step along the current one? Is this real darkness, or a passing shadow with much worse to come? Is this the great ordeal, or one of the many trials that lead up to it, training ground for the real challenge? If we knew when the story was due to end, we could work out where we are in the arc, as we do when we are reading a book or watching a drama on television or a film or play. You can see where, or know when, the story ends, so you can work out if this is the real denouement or if there is much more to come.

We don't know when this story of the coronavirus pandemic is going to end.

And although a great deal of educated planning can be done based upon scientific research and intelligence drawn from other places and times, this story, like all stories, is unique. It's frightening to think that things could get even tougher. How long can we bear to be in lockdown? Will we be able to cope with a second wave of infection? What is the 'new normal' to which we will have to adjust?

We can prepare as much as possible by anticipating scenarios, but we also have to prepare ourselves and our institutions for the unknown. We have to be like the medieval knights training their souls and bodies for quests that by definition they could not anticipate, trusting they would be ready to respond and adapt to they knew not what.

The quest we are embarked upon together is already testing our endurance. The trials are tough and long: key workers' arduous shifts in communities, care homes and hospitals; civil servants' production of coherent guidance at all hours; journalists' pressure to ensure stories are interrogated and then told truthfully; ministers' need to show steady, wise political leadership; parliament's need to scrutinise; citizens' often painful internal journeys in the long secluded hours of lockdown.

The response to the quest has been magnificent, but if we are to have enough strength to endure for an unknown length of time, we have to attend to ourselves.

The image I offer is of an archer, arrow held ready to let fly from the bow. The further back the archer draws the arrow, the further and more truly it will fly. We have to draw the bow back into whatever feeds our spirit to help it endure, as regularly and attentively as we eat and sleep and wash.

The question 'what strengthens my soul?' is a question for us all. Many answers are available, but the best answer for oneself becomes clear when the question is asked at depth. Stay with the question this week, keep asking it without rushing at an answer and, God willing, the letter next week will provide some suggestions that may have meaning for you.

You continue in our thoughts and prayers.

With love,
Claire

Letter seven: 7 May 2020

Unburdening your soul

Dear Friends,

You, public servants, and the different institutions through which you work, form a symphony of service that has never played so actively and fully as now. The music is sometimes being written barely moments before you play. How do you sustain your performance when you cannot be sure what the music will be, nor how long you will have to keep playing it?

I said last week that your soul needs to be strengthened if you are to continue to respond, serving the public, carrying the nation through this time of crisis and trial, however long it lasts, whatever unexpected challenges it presents.

One way of strengthening the soul is to release its burdens.

You serve with all your heart and that brings great fulfilment, but your service can weigh heavily on you. You relieve others of their troubles – in your online MP's surgery, say, or through your medical care, your advice to ministers, your truthful news article or your clarity of political leadership – but you can find that those troubles still hang about you, left behind in your heart when the one you have served has gone free. You carry the sweat and dirt of our nation. It can be painful.

You have to find ways of removing the sticky residue of your selfless service from your soul. Just saying rationally to yourself that there is no need to have this feeling doesn't, on its own, get rid of it. And in fact, as any therapist or confessor will tell you, you can't 'get rid' of the feeling at all. But, by recognising it is there and attending to it, it stops being damaging and can even become a source of creativity. A thousand different practices help, and you will find one that suits you. It may be walking in nature, or talking openly with trusted others, or going deep within yourself to find the quietude beyond the pain that allows the pain to release its grip.

I offer you the Ignatian* practice of feeling your way to your place of desolation. Sit quietly, breathe for a while to bring yourself to stillness, then imagine yourself on a careful interior journey to where you feel most tender and vulnerable. It is like seeing a dear friend before you who is in great pain. You cannot take away their pain, but you sit beside them and give them your attentive, loving company. You do not shun your vulnerability but wait with it, and it becomes life-giving.

There is another way in which the soul carries its burdens. Notions of how things should be done based on how they were done in the past can bind and blind us. The pandemic has presented completely new challenges, demanding responses that have no precedent. Unburdening our souls means loosening fixed perceptions and seeing afresh. To do so always needs the eyes of others who are not like us.

Diverse perceptions often initially make no sense to us. The voice that speaks quietly so you nearly miss it; if you're talking too loudly you drown it out, and if you're looking too hard

---

* St Ignatius of Loyola (1491–1556), founder of the Jesuits, from whose Spiritual Exercises this practice is drawn.

at one thing you can fail to notice the alternative view in the corner of your vision.

The divergent voice may come from among those obliged to keep away from active service, shielded through medical vulnerability, well placed in their stillness to see what others might be too busy to notice.

Wide open awareness and careful attention to the voices and perceptions of others keep the soul of the individual and the soul of the institution supple to respond to the new, as we need to now.

It would be good to make time this week to unburden your soul. Next week, God willing, this letter will offer you some food for it.

You continue in our thoughts and prayers.

With love,
Claire

Feeding your soul

Dear Friends,

You are all heroes in the story of the Covid-19 pandemic. You are heroes not because you have superhuman powers to save the world, but because, simply, you are protagonists. You undertake the labours the story demands of you, each in your own calling, with diligence and skill, but also with mixed motives and partial knowledge, with determination and a smile, but also with fear and grief in your hearts. You are fallible, and so are your institutions, and that makes your willingness to keep going through the story all the more impressive.

You can't control the story, but you can try to respond with the best that is in you, by strengthening your souls. Last week we sought to unburden them. This week we hope to feed them.

It's not so easy.

You, public servants, are not good at asking for yourselves. It is as if your time, none of it, is your own, and your needs, none of them, can come first. The attitude is sweet and honourable – and wrong. You must feed yourself in order to feed others and keep on feeding them.

The 'food' could be music or art or reading or prayer or dancing or laughing or silence or nature or conversation or a really absorbing film. For an institution, it could be giving employees time for any of the above; it could be trust, freely given and exercised with integrity; it could be properly delegated authority. The soul of an institution is fed if its people are fed.

Do you know what feeds your own soul? It might be similar to that which helps unburden your soul, just with a different focus. It should be a distinct, new act, like moving from washing your hands to eating a meal.

I cannot tell you what feeds your soul, only you can do that, but I can offer tests to help you to choose well.

Food for your soul is energising. If you come away from an activity depleted, then it is not food for your soul. It may be necessary for your public service but, if so, you must ensure you replace your energy with something that does feed you. Ask: is this activity, this company I am in, a radiator or a drain?

Food for your soul is lastingly nourishing. It is not junk food; it is fresh, good food. It is not grabbed and eaten on the go; it is prepared with love and served with grace. It leaves you deeply satisfied, not briefly stuffed. You don't hastily swallow without tasting; you savour every delicious mouthful.

Food for your soul is sufficient in itself. It is never utilitarian; it is never partaken in order to achieve something else; it is enough just to partake.

Food for your soul works obliquely. You partake out of love, not to make you a better person or change anything. And yet it strengthens you, and the world is better for it.

Food for your soul harms no one.

'Love bade me welcome,' wrote the seventeenth-century poet and priest George Herbert, 'but my soul drew back.' This week, draw forwards, find out what is food for your soul, and give yourself time to relish it, not as a duty, not as yet another burden, but because you love it with all your heart: 'Sit. And eat.'

Next week, God willing, the letter will offer some suggestions for exercising the soul.

You continue in our thoughts and prayers.

With love,
Claire

Letter nine: 22 May 2020

Exercising your soul

Dear Friends,

The weeks unfold and, with them, the story of the pandemic and our response to it. Your work continues unabated. The pressure is eased in some quarters and not in others, but your diligent attention has to be sustained – perhaps especially now, as people begin to move a little more freely again.

You must attend to the strength of your soul, your very self, if you are to sustain your steadfast service.

If your soul were a field, how would it feel? Fertile, or parched? Even if the exterior is dry and cracked, there will be moisture underneath. Unburdening and feeding our souls, the work proposed in the last two letters, could be thought of as turning the soil of our souls to soften them and prepare them to receive and germinate good seeds. Sowing good seeds is the exercise proposed in this week's letter.

The seeds I want to suggest sowing, while the coronavirus tests our endurance, are kindness, balance and patience. These seeds will not take root by wishful thinking alone, even if the ground is prepared. We have to act to sow them, but we can do this with surprisingly simple, physical movements.

Kindness can be summoned with a smile. However miserable you may feel, the physiological effort of stretching your cheek muscles changes your mood. It has to be a really big smile to work, like pushing the seed sufficiently far into the ground to ensure it will germinate. Smiling sows the seed of kindness in your soul. Keep doing it, even behind the mask covering your face. It will become a habit, and you will look more kindly on yourself and the world.

Balance starts as a physical feeling. Try standing or sitting still for a moment, and feel the ground beneath your feet. Send your attention downwards into the ground through your feet, following the seed, as it were, as you sow it all the way into the earth. Find the balance in your body supported by the earth and in doing so find it in your soul. Balance will generate a measured way of looking at your self and the world.

Patience can be evoked and practised by, quite simply, moving more slowly. Start when you're not in a hurry, and then choose deliberately to slow down when you *are* in a hurry. We all know the pressure of rushing from A to B, with the journey an infuriating necessity and everything and everyone you meet an obstacle to your arrival. In lockdown, the 'journey' sits between one activity and the next. Take time to pause between activities. Properly. Draw back from your computer and imagine you are carrying an orange between your shoulder blades.

Deliberately slowing your pace changes your perception as the seed of patience is sown deeply. Obstacles become encounters, often with beauty. You find time to welcome a stranger, even if it has to be in the form of a wave from a distance.

If St Paul is right, practising patience will generate the energy you need to persevere through these long weeks. And if you discover in yourself the steady strength to keep going, then hope will blossom.

Mother Julian of Norwich said that hell is despair, the complete absence of hope. So, whatever you are feeling, practise walking more slowly. Feel the ground supporting you beneath your feet, and smile at the world around you.

Next week, I hope to offer your souls some rest.

You continue in our thoughts and prayers.

With love,
Claire

Letter ten: 29 May 2020

Resting your soul

Dear Friends,

If you read a story in which the protagonist has to keep going for a long time, you can find yourself longing for the poor hero to be given a rest. You feel exhausted on their behalf. If the narrator doesn't attend to this, the narrative starts to lose plausibility because no one can keep going without a break. We are not automata.

Just as the silences between the notes are intrinsic to music, so rest between achievements is intrinsic to human flourishing. We know the importance of sleep, when brains process data, cells renew and bodies regain height. Sleep restores us: we can face almost anything after a good night's sleep, and almost nothing after a bad one. And the less we are able to come to rest during the day, the less we are likely to do so at night. Travelling physically between meetings gave us regular transition moments of rest, which online meetings, always in the same place and at the same computer, do not.

We are in danger, during the Covid-19 pandemic, of getting stuck in fight or flight mode, permanently in a state of heightened awareness, always in warrior pose, ready for action and reaction.

If you feel that the success of the response to the pandemic rests largely on your shoulders, or at the very least that if you let go for a moment of your bit of the response there will be dire consequences for others, then you are unlikely to be able to rest properly.

You may feel resentment that half the country is working its fingers to the elbow while the other half twiddles its thumbs. And if you can't serve as you wish to, your enforced stillness could be anything but relaxing.

How, then, can our minds stop buzzing and our hearts fall quiet? I have these suggestions to offer.

Try putting your service in perspective. A philosophical trick provides an analogy: how do you make a line shorter without doing anything to the line itself? You draw a longer line next to it. Place your service next to something bigger. Look at the stars hanging in the clear night skies and imagine the galaxy cradling our planet. See your place and purpose in a much bigger story.

Make a discipline of regularly relinquishing your claim on your work. Each of the great Abrahamic faith traditions has a sabbath. The principle of regular rest is a way to avoid pride, to recognise the smallness of one's contribution. The sabbath is the time not only to rest oneself but also to give everyone and everything else a rest from us. In some ways, nature has had a rest from us in these sabbath weeks of lockdown. Make sabbath time not just weekly, but between activities during the day.

Laugh at yourself. Find humour in your work. It might be gallows humour, but it helps.

Instead of the adrenalin-fuelled tension that leads to exhaustion, we can practise gently engaging our attention to our service, then releasing it, just as we might engage our muscles in exercise then release them. We can learn from the way fish move in the sea: they flap their fins when the waves flow in the direction they are going, and wait while the waves ebb. They do not try to fin against the flow. And for rest, they don't wait for the sea to stop, but dive deep beneath its waves and find its quiet centre.

In these ways we can keep going steadily for as long as we are called to do so. And we will emerge into whatever new worlds are waiting for us better equipped to flourish in them.

I invite you to attend to the practice of resting your soul this week. Next week, in the penultimate letter of this series, I will try to show further how the souls of institutions can be strengthened.

You continue in our thoughts and prayers.

With love,
Claire

Letter eleven: 5 June 2020

Strengthening the souls of institutions

Dear Friends,

The symphony of public service continues to respond to the pandemic, the music changing as circumstances change: tight, emphatic, staccato chords releasing tentatively into longer, sweeping notes as lockdown eases. You keep playing, and we remain grateful.

You play or sing your service as individuals, but the part you perform – the tenor line, say, or the second strings or the wind section – is given to you by virtue of the institution within which you work. And no matter how attentive, selfless and technically correct your service is, if the institution within which you offer it is off-key then your service too is compromised. So, it matters that our public service institutions of parliament, government, law, healthcare, education, faith, journalism and more are themselves able to attune to strong values and virtues.

Just as our own souls need strengthening to keep them supple and ready for service, so the 'souls' of our institutions do too.

If your soul is where your intrinsic value is to be found, it doesn't quite make sense to say that an institution has a soul. Institutions don't have intrinsic value; they are defined by their function. But an institution does have a personality, an emotional atmosphere that dictates the norms by which its workers act. This, which can be called its ethos, needs to be nurtured every bit as much as its efficiency. The ethos can give you energy or drain it from you. It can expect your best performance or condone your sloppiest. It can make you feel valued or exploited. It can be something you are supported by and can trust, or something you have to defend yourself against.

How do we tend to the ethos of an institution? Of course, you who lead it are responsible, but you may find it difficult – particularly in ancient, established institutions like those of our constitution. A negative ethos can stubbornly persist even when every job title and department has changed, even when every person who works in the institution has been replaced. And yet only *people* can enhance or modify the ethos. Leaders cannot do it alone: you have to empower your staff, all of them, by giving them some agency and the experience of their effective influence.

Over the last four weeks we have unburdened, fed, exercised and rested our own souls, and we can attend with the same readiness to the ethos of our institutions.

We can *unburden* them of old and painful baggage, which if ignored will carry on affecting all that the institution does. Unattended baggage is a reason why a negative ethos persists despite structural change. What are the stories the institution is holding on to? Tell them out in the light; find the creativity in their shadows.

We can *feed* the ethos with our institutions' better narratives: what are their histories, how can they inspire us now, and how can we add our chapter – the pandemic episode – so the story remains healthy and vibrant and inspires others in the future?

We can maintain an institution's ethical buoyancy through *exercising* our moral muscles, actively practising and rewarding integrity, patience and kindness, making the institution supple in its response to the unforeseeable and unknown.

We can recognise the importance of *rest* for a healthy ethos, and be determined to make time for it for all staff, time to switch off for long enough to quieten our buzzing minds and reconnect with the peace in our hearts, giving ourselves time to process grief, to address fear.

This week, I invite you to look up from playing your own instrument, notice the institutional ethos that is directly and indirectly influencing your performance, and see how you can in turn influence that ethos to the good.

You continue in our thoughts and prayers.

With love,
Claire

Letter twelve: 12 June 2020

A new level of life

Dear Friends,

This is the last letter in the series, written at a time of transition from crisis to living with a new reality. Now it is possible to look back and see a narrative arc emerging; one episode coming to a close even as another, much of it still unknown, begins. We can see, now, that the greatest ordeal fell on Easter weekend, when the press of patients in intensive care was at its most demanding.

The story is by no means over when the great ordeal is passed. The pace for many of you has been just as punishing since then; the relaxation of lockdown requires your vigilant attendance; for the most vulnerable, even more care has to be taken as the streets become busy again.

But in the classic plot line of the hero's quest, there is a time following the great ordeal when the protagonists draw breath, count the cost, and allow themselves to feel the gains of the journey. You can take a moment, now, to realise your greater strength and resilience, and reconnect with the deeper resources upon which you drew in order to undergo the ordeal. You know they are there because you felt them, and you can call upon them again. Joseph Campbell calls them the 'elixir', which is the real goal of the quest, not recognised until it is found, attained because of how we journeyed.

And having gained the elixir, you can both enjoy it and pass it on. This, in the story of the hero's quest, is a new level of life. The journey begins afresh, and we too are changed.

What have we learned, what can we bring into our new level of life, our unknown future?

Our leadership has been tested; we have felt the weight of it and the cost of it. The need to make unpopular decisions. The importance of giving one's word only when one can keep it. The acknowledgement that those who are idolised – the key workers – and those who face criticism – our political leaders – share a common humanity with us all. Fallible, yet motivated by public service. Fearful, and by the same token brave.

We learned that the human species is not at the top of the food chain. Our science knows all too well that we have to work with the grain of nature, not against it. We learned that we must live with the coronavirus; we will not defeat or obliterate it.

We learned to commune even as we distanced ourselves from each other. The distance allowed us to see each other more clearly, to give each other the space to be ourselves and exist in our own peace. And we learned that we are also porous to each other: my health depends on your health. I cannot seal myself off from you, so I must care for you. We learned that kindness is more important than almost anything.

We learned that the most valued members of our societies are those who enact love through care. These we cannot do without, and our economy has to arrange itself in service of humanity's care for one another and for the planet that provides us with food and shelter.

We learned humility, and gratitude. For simple, true things: birdsong; a tree trunk; eyes smiling above a mask.

We learned that the hero, in the hero's quest, is all of us.

I leave you with this image to sustain you in the next unfolding episode of the story. Birds catch thermals, a bank of warm air that supports them on the wing, which they can ride, resting even as they move. Find your thermal: that sweet spot, when you relax into your work, your skill, your vocation, and feel supported by the response from those you serve. You need to be supported. You need to feel that you are not alone, that the burden doesn't rest solely on your shoulders. Find your thermal, and ride it. Fly!

You will continue in our thoughts and prayers.

With love,
Claire

Learning to Dance Through the Rain:
A Police Officer's Perspective

Treena Fleming

Some weeks before Covid-19 and the lockdown really took hold, I had asked my staff officer, Ross, to block out a week in my diary, delegate any meetings to my deputy and call it my 'People Week'. The purpose of it was to spend some time with my BCU* officers and staff, check in with them, have a chat over a cup of tea and listen to their concerns and ideas. At the time, I did not realise how significant that week would become. It turned into the week that lockdown commenced.

Responding to an emergency is what we are good at in the Metropolitan Police Service (MPS). In fact, you might say that we thrive on a crisis, as our innate leadership qualities kick in and we get a chance to do what we joined up for – to help our most vulnerable at their greatest time of need and 'catch the baddies'! Of course, this crisis was a little different, and it concerned a 'baddie' many of us had not encountered before... This was a public health emergency, a pandemic, and it had already

---

* BCU stands for Basic Command Unit. The Metropolitan Police Service maps its 32 London police boroughs into 12 Basic Command Units, each made up of between two and four boroughs.

claimed many lives throughout the world. On a daily basis, I am humbled by the resourcefulness and tenacity of my officers and staff to get the job done. A recent pre-pandemic commendation ceremony brought a smile to my face when I learned that my officers were not to be deterred from answering a 999 call after their police car had broken down: they simply answered it on the back of a tow truck en route to the garage!

However, this particular emergency was one in which my brave officers and staff were vulnerable too. Some colleagues had tragically already lost loved ones to this terrible disease, and I worried that I might see this dreadful illness claiming the lives of my much loved, dependable workforce. But it's really not that easy to find many roles in the police service where you are able to work from home. I thought long and hard about what we might have to stop doing for our communities and the residents of North Area,* and when we might have to stop doing it. My senior leadership team and I became obsessed with monitoring the rising sickness rates at our daily management meetings to determine whether we had reached 'the next level' and needed to start brigading our resources. I followed the MPS Commissioner's lead and split my leadership team so that they were working from different locations, knowing that there would be resilience and a back-up plan should any of us fall ill.

When you become a BCU Commander, you feel a great sense of responsibility for the area you police, the communities you serve, and the officers and staff that you lead. During that first week of the lockdown – my People Week – and for

* North Area comprises the two police boroughs of Enfield and Haringey.

the weeks following, it was crucial that my teams saw me. I wanted them to know that I was at their side and that we were going through this together. I knew that the one service we had to provide at all costs was an emergency response, so that we were able to answer that 999 cry for help from a child witnessing domestic abuse or an elderly couple fearful for their safety because someone was trying to break in. My concern was that the sickness levels among my officers would rise so rapidly that even this basic level of public service would not be achievable. Of course, we had well-rehearsed contingency plans in place, which even looked at how we'd brigade resources among the BCUs, but no one wanted to reach this strange, unfamiliar level of service.

Personal circumstances meant that I was separated from family members during the lockdown, and at times it was lonely and incredibly frustrating that I couldn't be united with them at such a difficult time. But I found my strength in knowing that near on 600,000 residents were looking to myself and the North Area team to lead them through this uncertainty, and the feeling of loneliness lessened as the sense of duty took over. I turned up, armed with biscuits, at parade bases where officers gather for their roll call and intelligence briefing at the start of every shift, and found the banter and smiling faces infectious. I chuckled at the resourceful sergeant who was trading eggs for some other valuable commodity they had not been able to source. Precious moments such as these were the motivation and inspiration I needed to remain focused on leading my teams through the crisis.

While on parade – our roll call and briefing – I listened to their concerns about taking the illness back to their pregnant

partner or elderly relative. I hoped my words of encouragement would spur them on. I told them how proud I was that
they had put their own fears to one side so that we could continue to police Enfield and Haringey. I explained that many of
our communities would be feeling frightened and uncertain
of the future. It was our job to remain stoic and to guide and
reassure them through the crisis. I set the tone for our policing
style – the four Es (engage, explain, encourage and, as a very
last resort, enforce) – and I advised that it had never been more
important to win the support of our communities, to bring
them with us. At a time when personal frustrations within our
communities would be heightened, I wanted my officers to
police with empathy and kindness. I did not want our years of
enhanced community engagement to be eroded by one over-
zealous fixed penalty notice and, most importantly, I wanted
to instil a sense of social responsibility in North Area whereby
we understood that *together* we would save lives: our communities alongside our police officers.

Crime levels and call demand did fall. I remember the bit-
tersweet feeling when we reached zero robberies in a 24-hour
period. I had dreamt of this day since I first took over as the
BCU Commander in April 2019, but so much human suffering
was attached to it that I could not celebrate and it was quickly
forgotten. I remember driving around the BCU with Ross
as we travelled between parade sites. Once busy and vibrant
North Area streets were now eerily deserted. At the parade
sites, Ross became accustomed to me using the words 'national
emergency' and 'unprecedented times' in team briefings. On
one occasion, I stood with the MPS Chaplain at Quicksilver
patrol base in Haringey, which predominantly houses our

emergency response officers in the south of the BCU. He had come to offer his support to the team (not the last rites, as one inspector cheekily suggested) and our hearts were warmed as we witnessed the committed faces and camaraderie of our officers and staff. Covid-19 could not deter them from their efforts to get on with the job, as we dealt with the two shootings and the tragic murder that had recently occurred on the BCU.

We were cheered on in our work by local councillors and MPs who sent us words of encouragement and praise. We were touched by community acts of kindness: local gin distilleries and breweries made us hand sanitiser when we ran short, local businesses left us food parcels, and bakeries and anonymous callers left us beautiful cakes on the station steps to say thank you. We are indebted to the schoolteachers who took our children in so that we could carry on policing the BCU. North Area criminals were even allegedly contributing to the effort by observing the guidelines and insisting on social distancing during drug deals.

In the end, we never had to pause any area of policing on North Area, such was the resilience, professionalism and calibre of my officers, staff and senior leadership team. Things have changed for us as a police service: we have embraced virtual meetings, the concept of agile working has firmly landed in our psyche, and auspicious occasions such as passing out parades and long service ceremonies have plummeted. However, what has not changed is the commitment, selflessness and dedication to duty that I observed in abundance throughout this crisis. I have nothing but respect and admiration for my courageous colleagues in North Area and beyond.

Lessons in Resilience: An MP's Perspective

Dawn Butler

At the beginning of lockdown I had this fantasy, like a lot of other people, that I would have time to tidy my house, give it a spring clean, pick up my violin and learn to play it again, and rest my soul, as Claire's letters suggested. How could I have known that my lockdown was going to be filled with so much sad, sad news? Like many others, my every morning – once with its routine of getting ready, having an hour's trip into work, speaking to my niece, and touching base – was disrupted. As soon as I got up, there was no need to do all of the getting ready if I didn't want to; I could just have a quick shower and put on a top half for the meetings. I would roll out of bed and on to the computer, and there I would stay until I was called by the grumblings of my belly to get something to eat. And I would not leave the computer until 9 or 10 o'clock at night, when I'd held all the evening meetings in addition to the day meetings. I *had* to keep going into the evenings: I could feel the desperation in the voices of the people who asked.

I had constituents stranded all over the world, some in places I'd never even heard of. They were trying to get home, and I had to struggle hard with the government to try to get them home. I could not understand why we couldn't do this better. It played on my soul every single day, and I ended up, when I finally went to bed, not being able to sleep because I worried about my constituents, I worried about the emails I was being sent, I worried that we weren't caring enough as a country to sort out everyone's problems and get them home safely.

Every day I had a tsunami of bad news. As well as people stranded abroad, the death rate in my constituency of Brent was going up. I was speaking confidentially to doctors who told me, in much more depth than anything available to the public, of the way the virus was behaving and the strange multifold symptoms it was producing in their patients. The virus was clever, they told me: it was mutating, attacking the brain, the heart, the lungs, the kidneys. I had to digest that information and manage my role as a Member of Parliament and as a member of society. It was quite a heavy burden. In addition, my staff struggled. They have been with me from the beginning, and they're very dependent on each other, so isolation was hard. And it wasn't straightforward: some of them only had Wi-Fi on their phones, or their laptops hardly worked. Some of them are single parents or they live in shared houses. One member of staff lived in his bedroom for the entire period: all of a sudden, his bedroom was his office, the place where he slept, his entertainment, his pub. We had to get laptops and internet boosters, even a desk and chair. I felt keenly how unfair was the criticism of MPs for receiving £10,000 to manage our offices in lockdown. The money wasn't for me, it was for my staff.

In addition to their logistical challenges, my staff suffered with lack of sleep, depression, skin problems, and Covid-19 itself – one staff member had the virus more than once. And in addition they were dealing with my hate mail. There was a lot of abuse, more than normal, heightened because of the pandemic. I received over 2,000 individual messages of hate via social media and email. I cope by not reading most of them, but my staff have to read them because they have to report them to the police and the police have to investigate. My staff's reaction was hard to see; their reactions were intensified by the pandemic and their emotions got me emotional, so that I can hardly bear to write about it.

On top of wave after wave of the grief my constituents were suffering and sharing with me, Covid-19 hit my own family. My uncle died of it. He had reached a good age, but it was hard not being there because we're a big family and we grieve together. His only son, Johnny, had died just a few weeks earlier, so the grief was compounded. It felt like an overload of grief; too much to handle. Media outlets wanted me to talk about it. I couldn't share or talk about it. Then my auntie's husband fell sick. His son came over to look after him, and died. Then my auntie's husband died. There was more grief, more pain that couldn't be shared, that had to be processed alone by all of us.

Because I'm an MP, people think I know what the government is doing. But I'm in opposition, not in government. My job in parliament is to hold government to account; I'm not on the inside at cabinet meetings hearing all the decisions. I was receiving letters and emails full of questions and a lot of fake news, but I understood that most people were experiencing a gap between what was happening to them and what the government was telling them, so they filled that space with their own consciousness or conspiracy. And sometimes they were right, and sometimes they were very much off the mark. I couldn't bridge the gap for them: I didn't know myself. How could I build resilience in them?

And then: eight minutes and 46 seconds happened. The brutal killing and lynching of George Floyd. I watched maybe a minute of it, but I knew how it ended; I'd seen it so many times before. I'd become almost jaded by that kind of death. But then people started to react. The killing couldn't be explained away by saying that George Floyd was violent; he was resisting arrest, and so a police officer decided to kneel on his neck. The officer had his hand in his pocket, adding extra weight to his knee as he cut off the circulation in Floyd's windpipe. The camera spanned around, and you could see two or three other police officers kneeling on him. You couldn't explain this brutal act of racism by saying that Floyd was struggling and resisting arrest now.

This very public lynching was about to open up generational wounds and generational trauma, for me personally and for many others, and it was about to start a discussion on racism, one that I've had many times from as young an age as I can remember. Just as I thought I was going to be able to rest a little from the pandemic's grief and work and support and hate mail and pressure, I had to take a deep breath and allow my voice to become public. I wasn't planning to say anything I hadn't said before, but now people were listening and hearing in the stillness of the pandemic.

Structural and systemic racism has existed for 400 or 500 years. It's a social construct designed to allow one group of human beings to dehumanise another based on the easily seen colour of a person's skin. It is designed to make one group of people feel superior and another inferior. If you don't believe me, believe the Covid-19 body count: there's no reason why the death toll is so much higher in black African, Caribbean,

Asian and minority ethnic people. Covid-19 doesn't prefer one person's set of lungs to another's: we're all from the human race. It's not the virus that discriminates, it's society.

My mother taught me resilience; my brothers taught me resistance. My mother sent me to school in the morning saying to myself: sticks and stones will break my bones, but words will never hurt me. I would skip along the road to school singing that tune. But the fights I had in school happened because the other children were calling me names. It wasn't true that words didn't hurt. My brothers taught me: 'Sis, if you're in trouble, don't call the police, call us. We will come and we will help you. The police won't help you.' I'd heard the stories about how the police treated my brothers. When I started driving, my brothers told me to look in my mirror when a police car drove past, and if they turned around to follow me, to make sure I stopped in a very public place. These were the resistance tools that my brothers were teaching me. I realise now that what my parents were teaching me was resilience, and this is how they coped. They had a form of resilience to survive to get us here, and my generation was retaliating and fighting. Now the new generation has all of that plus social media, worldwide connection, and that makes their movement – this generation's movement – different.

When I was younger, I went to a party in my new car. The neighbour was upset by the party, and he came out with a brick and he threw the brick through my car window. When I was told about this I went and knocked on the neighbour's door. He came out with another brick. I thought, I'm going to get hurt, and I called my brothers. They came to help me, and one of my brothers knocked on the neighbour's door. This time he came out with a knife. I thought, he's going to kill my brother, and I called the police. The first thing the police did was to arrest my brother. I thought they were moving him to safety, but they weren't. I started screaming hysterically: '*I* called you, why are you not helping me?' It made no difference; they weren't going to let my brother go, they were arresting him. So I said, 'You have to arrest this man too. He's got the knife: look at him, he's got the knife.' Eventually the police turned around and saw the knife and arrested the white man. And I thought to myself, as my brother was carted away in the police van: I'm going to get my brother killed. He *told* me not to call the police.

In the middle of lockdown, in the aftermath of the George Floyd killing, I spoke to my brother. Did he remember the incident? He said: 'Remember it, Sis? I still have the scars.' I thought he meant the mental scars. But he meant the scars he had on his wrists from the handcuffs that cut off his circulation and made his wrists bleed. He said that when the police threw him in the back of the car, they knelt on him, they put their feet on him, so when he watched George Floyd dying, he thought: that could have been me. I was in tears. He was confirming my worst fears: that that day, I could have got my brother killed – not by the white guy with the knife but by the police.

This is not about the police. The police often help me and protect me, not least by dealing with my hate mail. The majority of police officers are good, but this is about systemic and systematic racism.

Resilience comes from the Latin meaning rebound, recoil, the mental ability to recover quickly from misfortune, illness or depression. Somehow, in lockdown, we have had to find and build our resilience, and we have to keep learning. John Lewis, the congressman and freedom fighter who passed away in July 2020, said: 'We used to say that ours is not the struggle of one day, one week, or one year. Ours is the struggle of a lifetime, or maybe even many lifetimes, and each one of us in every generation must do our part. And if we believe in the change we seek, then it is easy to commit to doing all we can, because the responsibility is ours alone to build a better society and a more peaceful world.' I don't know how this journey will end, but I think that what we will take from this time will be that systemic and systematic racism needs to end, and each and every one of us has to call it out. Because it clouds everything that we do.

Right at the beginning of lockdown, I wrote this poem:

Why does everything have to be about race?
Why can't you just let people be people?
And you, know your place.
When you think about it
It's a simple thing to say.
But will 'let people be people' really
Wash racism away?
If we had equity rather than equality,
Would that be a more level playing field?
Would the death rate of Covid have led
To fewer black people to shield?
The truth is
Privilege or ignorance
Often make you blind to see
The injustice that's plain to see.

Symphony of Service: A Civil Servant's Perspective

Peter Howitt

When, at the end of February, I was told I needed to return to the Department of Health and Social Care to work on the response to Covid-19, I was torn. On the one hand, I could see Covid-19 was going to become a huge public health challenge. On the other hand, I had just been offered a promotion to extend my secondment in the NHS. Was I, one civil servant among many, so crucial?

On my own I was not irreplaceable, but as part of the department's Incident Response Team I have been one of over a hundred civil servants who have been collectively vital. Vital in providing the daily data on those who have died in the pandemic. Vital in bringing home hundreds of Britons holidaying on cruise ships. Vital in providing guidance to underpin the 'new normal' of social distancing. The image Claire has painted in her letters of public service as an orchestra is apt, with individual contributions combining to create collective achievements, just as individual musicians create a complete symphony.

It has always been the case that the best thing about the Civil Service is the people. In this crisis, that truth has been amplified. The Department of Health and Social Care has needed more staff working on Covid-19 than it had available. And so civil servants from trade and tax, education and employment have volunteered to help in this task. They have pitched up with no notice and got straight on with sorting out complex issues. It has shown that, despite departmental loyalties, the Civil Service truly can act as one when faced with grave national challenges. This sense of collective endeavour has undoubtedly helped give me the energy and resilience to cope with difficult tasks, such as reporting the deaths of the third and fourth people to die of Covid-19 in the UK or trying to find a route home for holidaymakers on board a cruise ship that no port would accept.

Reporting individual deaths feels an age away as I write this in mid-June when the death toll is over 40,000. At the time, there was intense media interest in each tragic individual case and, once the family was notified, it was important to coordinate the announcement by the hospital with an acknowledgement from the Chief Medical Officer to the nation. For the cruise ship, there was the worry that while Covid-19 cases on board were currently limited, any unnecessary delay in getting people off the ship could lead to an outbreak. There were other health considerations too, including the need to get prescription medication to passengers whose supplies had run out. We needed to get people home quickly and safely, and this required logistics to resupply the ship and diplomacy to find somewhere the passengers could disembark. In both these cases, I was dependent on the input of others: the NHS, our press office and the Chief Medical Officer's team for death reporting; the Foreign and Commonwealth Office, Department of Transport and others for the cruise ship. This sharing of responsibilities with other public servants made it easier to do things that a few weeks previously would have seemed fanciful.

The word 'love' in the Western mindset has become focused on romantic relationships, but I, like many civil servants, am motivated by a love for our neighbours. The concept of our response to Covid-19 as being about love, not war, as eloquently set out in Claire's fourth letter, resonates with me. I do care about my fellow citizens and want to do the best I can for them. Sharing that caring impulse with others in the department is certainly a powerful driver to keep you going through difficult conversations and competing pressures.

On a more prosaic level, working as part of a shift system 07:00–22:00, seven days a week, has made the task much more manageable. Although a strain on my sleep patterns and social engagements, working in shifts has meant that I have effectively been part of a three-way job share. To use a sporting analogy to complement the musical one, I have been able to pass on the baton. But, as spectators of the 4 × 100 metres relay will know, it is at the point of transfer where there is greatest risk of disaster. I had to become adept at the succinct handover that covered the crucial issues for the next Incident Director coming on to shift. This role sharing has meant that, while I have had some very early starts and fewer evenings to catch up on Netflix boxsets, I have not been glued to my emails while off shift. I have also had time in the week to support the homeschooling of my sons. Contrary to the situation outlined in letter ten, the inability to rest, I *have* been able to focus elsewhere, secure in the knowledge that the necessary work is continuing. For me, the need for more of a sense of shared responsibility, rather than individual heroic efforts, is a key theme that has come out of this extraordinary time.

One example of shared responsibility, and a very established one in the Civil Service, is the committee. Committees often elicit groans, but I have been privileged to be the departmental sponsor of our Moral and Ethical Advisory Group, a committee that brings together clinicians, health ethicists and religious representatives. Not able to meet in person, the group has grappled with complex issues over the phone, such as how to conduct funerals in the era of Covid-19. How do you strike the correct balance between protecting public health and allowing people to mourn the passing of loved ones? Always respectful of the diverse views offered by others, the group has helped shape guidance, bringing a moral and ethical perspective to policymaking.

Letter eight explored the food for your soul that keeps you going in difficult times. Beyond my work and supporting it, I would point to three things: family, friends and faith. The support of my wife and sons has been brilliant throughout. For my children, when I had my career quandary at the start of this story, the correct answer was always that I should be working to mitigate the impact of the coronavirus. Virtual quizzes and boardgames with friends have provided light relief and distraction from the growing death toll and challenges in the office. And my faith, a belief in a loving God who is in control, provides reassurance when the news is bleak and unrelenting.

Faith, friends and family. I know that emphasising the importance of these three things is hardly original or insightful. Yet I think the Covid-19 situation has helped to strip away the ephemera of modern life and enabled me to think about what really matters.

Reflecting on my coronavirus experience to date has happened at the same time as I have moved to lead a team that is empowered to consider how the department has dealt with coronavirus. This looking back is not about blame or acclaim. It is about how we can be better next time. What do we need to do differently ahead of a potential second peak of Covid-19? How do we prepare for other major incidents that will affect our nation's health? This plays into wider questions that Claire touches upon in her letters. How can we build a better Civil Service, a better public service, a better society out of the upheaval of the last few months? Successfully answering this question must be the legacy of the crisis we have faced.

Westminster Abbey Institute

Letters from Lockdown: Sustaining Public Service Values During the Covid-19 Pandemic is published in partnership with Westminster Abbey Institute. The Institute was founded by Westminster Abbey in 2013 to work with the people and institutions by whom it is surrounded in Parliament Square, to revitalise moral and spiritual values and virtues in public life. It offers space and time for challenging lectures, conversations, ideas and quiet reflection.

In doing so, the Institute aims to remind those who govern of their vocation to public service, helping them to grow in moral sensitivity and resilience and to better define the good they are trying to do.

The material in this book does not necessarily represent the views of Westminster Abbey or its Institute.